W9-CLC-142

This Book

presented to the

CHURCH LIBRARY IN MEMORY OF

Mother of T.C. Freedman

BY

Birdville Baptist Church

Code 4386-23, No. 3, Broadman Supplies, Nashville, Tenn. Printed in USA

Presented

to

_____

_____

by

_____

_____

_____
DATE

GOOD MORNING, LORD

Devotions for Children

Dena Korfker

Baker Book House
Grand Rapids, Michigan

Copyright © 1973 by
Baker Book House Company

ISBN: 0-8010-5328-5

Published in the United States of America

To
My present and last
class of kindergarten pupils
at Oakdale Christian
with all my love

SOMETHING TO REMEMBER
A NOTE TO MOTHERS

Children find security in very simple things. Have you ever heard your child boast, "We always go to grandmother's on Sunday afternoon," or "My daddy always reads me a story before I go to bed," or "We always have hot dogs for supper on Saturday night"? Children like to remember the habitual things that happen in their home. It makes them feel safe. And when they are grown, they will look back with nostalgia on those very things.

I have a friend whose family was very poor when she was a girl. Their breakfast consisted of a slice of toast with butter and a glass of milk. But on Sunday they had a special treat—a little sugar sprinkled over the toast. Although my friend is no longer poor and can eat what she wishes, a slice of toast with sugar is still a treat for her.

What I am trying to say is, the things we do as children go with us all through life. What better legacy can you give your child than the habit of spending some part of each day together in close communion with his heavenly Father. Not only will it give him something good to remember, it will start him on the right road that leads to Christian living.

The short devotions in this book were written to help your child become more aware of the constant, abiding presence of his Lord and Savior. It is my earnest prayer that Jesus may become as real to your child as the things he can see and touch, so that he may soon learn that Jesus is far more important than anything this world has to offer.

Dena Korfker

1 GOOD MORNING, LORD

In the morning, You hear my voice, O Lord; in the morning I prepare a prayer for You and watch and wait for You to speak to my heart. —Psalm 5:3, *The Amplified Bible*

Once there was a little girl named Selma. She lived on a farm in North Dakota. Selma lived in the days when there were no furnaces to heat the homes. The only warm place in her home was the kitchen, close to the big cook stove.

Selma's bedroom was upstairs. It was very cold up there, and it wasn't much fun to get up in the morning. Her bed was so cozy and warm. Selma would screw up her courage for a moment, then jump out of bed, dash across the cold floor with her bare feet, and scurry downstairs to the warm kitchen stove.

But before Selma made her wild dash each morning, she always took time to talk for a few moments with her best Friend, Jesus, her Savior. She would always tell Him how much she loved Him. She would ask Him to help her be a good girl. She would tell Him the things that made her happy and the things that made her afraid. And she would always end her talk with these words, "Come, Lord Jesus, take my hand, and walk with me the whole day through."

What a wonderful way to begin a new day! Is getting-up time a bad time at your home? Try Selma's way. Don't wait for mother and dad to get cross with you. Ask your parents to buy you an alarm clock so you can wake up by yourself. As soon as you hear the alarm bell, say, "Good Morning, Lord." Then thank Him for your good night and for letting you wake up to a new day. Thank Him for all His wonderful gifts to you. Talk over your plans for the day, and ask for His help. Stay close to Jesus all day. Then you will have a good day.

2   JESUS KNOWS THE WAY

You know my path. —Psalm 142:3
You will show me the path of life.
—Psalm 16:11
O my God, I trust in You. —Psalm 25:3

Peter was blind. He had never seen all the lovely things in our world which we see every day. He didn't know how beautiful the flowers look in the garden on a sunny day in June. He didn't know how lovely a rainbow looks when the sun shines through the rain. Peter didn't even know what a smile was like! But do you think Peter didn't know when his mother was smiling at him? Oh, yes, he knew! He just let his other four senses teach him what he couldn't learn through his eyes. God gave us five wonderful senses: seeing, hearing, smelling, tasting, and touching. All these five gifts help us learn and bring us joy.

Peter loved to walk through the garden with his father. His father would guide his hand and help him "see" through the touch of his fingers what the flowers were like. His ears would tell him what the brook was like. And his nose would tell him the difference between a rose and a lilac.

One day a friend of his father came into the garden. He watched Peter and his father and said, "Peter, aren't you afraid to walk when you cannot see where you are going?" Peter shook his head, "No, I'm not afraid. I do not know the way by myself, but my father does. And he's holding my hand!"

Peter trusted his father completely. He knew that his father loved him and would never let anything bad happen to him. Do you know what trust means? You can trust your heavenly Father, just as Peter trusted his father. Your heavenly Father knows the way you have to go. Trust in Him and you will never have to be afraid.

3   NO OTHER WAY

*Listen to and obey My voice, and I will
be your God and you will be My people.*
—Jeremiah 7:23, *The Living Bible*

This is the chorus of a favorite song of God's
children:

> Trust and obey,
> For there's no other way
> To be happy in Jesus,
> But to trust and obey.

We have talked about *trust.* When we trust
someone, we feel perfectly safe with him. We
know he loves us and will take good care of us.
We trust Jesus because He has promised to give
us everything we need—always! But the song
says we must *trust* and *obey.* Do you know what
obey means? When we obey someone, we do
what he tells us to do. And we do not do what
he tells us not to do.

It isn't easy to obey. It is much easier *not* to
obey. Even though we love our parents and want
to please them, we so quickly forget their rules.
It takes a lot of thinking and remembering to be
obedient.

And sometimes we don't even feel like obeying! We want to do what is wrong. That's because there is sin in our hearts. But if you are a

Christian—that means that you love Jesus and believe that He is your Savior—then you do not have to give in to sin. Jesus will help you learn to obey. And it will give you much happiness when you do!

4   HAPPY AS A LARK

I will sing to the Lord as long as I live; I will sing praise to my God while I have any being. —Psalm 104:33

Have you ever seen or heard a lark? A lark is a rather small bird. He looks something like an ordinary sparrow. But when he flies, he is a sight to behold! He swoops and darts and soars high into the sky. (This is why he is often called a skylark.) And as he flies, he sends down to you his most delightful song! His tiny throat fairly bursts with melody. Your whole world seems filled with the sound of his singing. And you go on your way with a happy heart.

There is something which brings even more happiness to the hearts of people than the song of a bird. It is the singing of people. I think God must love music very much. He sort of built it right into His children when He made them. One of the first things a baby learns to do is to hum little sounds to himself. And by the time he is two or three he is already making up little songs and singing some of the songs his mother sings to him.

And when babies grow into children, and children become grown-ups, they soon learn that singing is a wonderful way to show what they feel. God is very happy when He hears His children praising Him when they are in church. He likes to hear them singing at home and at school too. In the olden days, when the Bible-people lived, music was very important. David and others wrote 150 songs which they called psalms. They used these when they praised God in church. And whenever something special happened, they wrote a song about it.

Are you as happy as a lark? Do you make your home a happy place by the songs you sing? Let David's song be yours today—"I will sing to the Lord as long as I live."

5 HOW DO I SHOW MY LOVE FOR JESUS?

Stop being mean, bad-tempered, and angry. Quarreling, harsh words, and dislike of others should have no place in your lives. Instead, be kind to each

*other, tenderhearted, forgiving one an-
other, just as God has forgiven you because you belong to Christ.* —Ephesians
4:32,32, *The Living Bible*

If someone were to ask you, "Do you love
Jesus?" you would answer, "Yes, of course I
love Jesus." But if you were asked, "How can
you show me that you love Jesus?" what would
you answer?

Do you know the story of the little boy who
wished Jesus would come to visit him in his
home? He said he wished Jesus would be about
the same size he was, and just as old—which was
five. He would let Him sit in his own little
rocking chair. They would have milk and cook-
ies together. Then they would play together.
And he would let Jesus have any toy He wished.
He could be first at any game. And before Jesus
went away, he would let Him choose any toy He
wanted to take home for His very own.

As the little boy sat thinking, he said, "I
know Jesus can't come to me as a little boy, but
I could show my love for Him by letting Johnny
sit in my rocking chair. I could share my toys
with Peter and Bill. I could let Mary be first
when we play my new game, and perhaps I
should let Michael choose one of my toys for his
very own. He doesn't have any toys to play
with."

This little boy in my story must have heard of the lovely rule Jesus gave to His people when He was here on this earth. Jesus said if we do something kind to someone else because we love Him, we are really doing it to Him.

So, how can you show your love for Jesus? Begin in your own home. Don't fight with your brothers and sisters. Try sharing what you have and what you are with those around you.

6   THE TOUCH OF JESUS

And they kept bringing young children to Him, that He might touch them. . . . And He took the children up in His arms one by one, and blessed them, placing His hands upon them. —Mark 10:13,16, *The Amplified Bible*

You remember one morning we talked about our five senses. If we could not see or hear or smell or taste or touch, we would have no way of learning anything. We would have no way of reaching out to other people or to anything in this world. Do you remember to thank God every day for your five senses?

Let's talk about the sense of touch. If we

could not feel with our fingers, we would not be able to make beautiful things or play beautiful music.

There is something even more important about the sense of touch. Through touch we show our feelings. We show love by throwing our arms around someone or by holding his hand. We can often express our feelings better through touch than with words.

When Jesus lived on this earth, people were always crowding around Him to touch Him. Every day Jesus touched the sick and they became well. Sometimes He took a dead person by the hand and made him alive again. He touched children and babies. He held them in His arms and made them very, very happy.

When Jesus lived on earth with His body, He could touch only one person at a time. He could be in only one place at a time. Today He lives in our hearts with His Spirit. We cannot see Him or understand this, but it is true. He touches all of His children every day. He makes you feel that He is with you and loves you in many ways.

7   A WONDERFUL TREASURE

*Your Word is a lamp to my feet and a
light to my path.* —Psalm 119:105

> I have a wonderful treasure,
> The gift of God without measure,
> And so we travel together—
> My Bible and I.

Do you know what it means to have a treasure? A treasure is something you like very
much and want to keep forever. You do not
want anyone to take it away from you. The
Bible is a wonderful treasure! There is nothing in
the world that is more important to own than a
Bible.

If the Bible had never been written, we
would know very little about God. We would
know that there *was* a God, because we can tell
that from the wonderful world He has made.
You can't make a flower, you can't make a tree,
you can't even make a tiny, wiggly caterpillar,
nor change him into a beautiful butterfly. Only
God can do these things.

But you could enjoy God's many wonders in
His beautiful world for a thousand years and still
never find out about Jesus. You might learn that
there was sin in this world, because you would
see what sin has done to God's lovely world.
You would notice how some animals fight and

kill other animals. You would see how tiny little bugs make strong, beautiful trees wither and die. And you know that sometimes people kill and hurt each other.

You need the Bible to tell you about Jesus. The Bible tells you how Jesus came from heaven to live and die so that He could take away the sins of His people. Everything you need to know about yourself and about God is in that Bible. It is your finest treasure!

8   MY BIBLE

Your Word have I hid in my heart, that I might not sin against you. —Psalm 119:11

Is there a Bible in your home? Where do you keep it? How often is it used? Owning a Bible is important, but it is not enough. A Bible on the bookshelf does no one any good. If the Bible is to be our guide in life, each member in the family should have a Bible of his own as he becomes old enough to read. Then he will be able to read the Bible by himself and hear God speak to him alone.

You may be too young to read the Bible by

yourself, but there are many lovely books which tell all the stories from the Bible. Ask your father or your mother to read one of those stories to you every night before you go to bed. Then you can hear God talking to you, too; and you will know what the Bible is all about even before you learn to read!

And how should the Bible be read? Like you would read a letter from daddy if he was away from home for a week or so. Your mother would gather all the children together, and she would read the letter very carefully, so as not to miss a word. Then she would read it again, and perhaps again, until you knew it all by heart. God's Book is like a long letter from your dear heavenly Father. In it He tells you all about Himself: what He has done, what He is doing, and how much He loves you. He also tells you what you must do. He shows you how to live.

Even if you cannot read God's Book, you can learn some of it by heart. Begin by learning today's verse. The more you learn from God's Word, the more you will love Him and want to live for Him.

9 SAVED FROM THE LIONS

Then Daniel said to the king, "O king, live forever! My God has sent His angel and has shut the lions' mouths so that they have not hurt me." —Daniel 6:21,22

Do you remember the story of the brave young man Daniel, who wouldn't pray to his king? Some wicked men who were jealous of Daniel tricked the king into making a new rule that no one was allowed to pray to anyone except the king. And the punishment for disobeying the rule was to be thrown to the lions. Daniel had to disobey because he loved God and wouldn't worship anyone else. So Daniel was thrown into the lions' den. But did the lions eat him? Oh, no! Daniel trusted God to save him; and God sent His angel to keep Daniel safe, even in a lions' den!

Do you think God would help a boy or a girl in such a way today? Not many years ago, God did answer a girl's prayer and saved her from the lions!

Deep in the jungles of Africa, lived a girl named Xide (Zee-da). She heard the story of Jesus from a missionary, and believed in Him. Her parents were very angry and tried to make her stop being a Christian. They beat her! But the more they hurt her, the more Xide prayed to Jesus for strength. Finally, because she didn't know what else to do, her mother took her out to the jungle and tied her to a tree. That night Xide asked God to deliver her from the lions that were coming to the tree. She could see the fire in their eyes as they came closer. They roared at her. They walked around her tree. They even sat down on the soft earth and watched her. But they never came close enough to touch her!

In the morning a Christian boy came by. He loosened Xide and brought her to the missionary. Together they went back to the tree and saw the paw marks where the lions had walked. They could even see where the lions had sat down to watch Xide. God kept His child Xide safe, too.

Do you ever ask God to make your faith strong like Daniel's?

10   KEEP YOUR CONSCIENCE SHARP

A man's mind plans his way, but the Lord directs his steps and makes them sure. —Proverbs 16:9

Do you know what a conscience is? Everyone is born with a conscience. When God made

Adam and Eve, He made them perfect. They knew in their own minds that what they thought or said or did was good and right. After man sinned, he still kept his conscience. He still knew whether his thoughts or words or acts were good or bad. Your conscience is a gift from God to help you choose the good instead of the bad. He wants you to keep your conscience in good working order.

That means you have to be careful with your conscience. The first time you do something wrong—perhaps you take some money from your mother's purse or you copy your work from the other children in school instead of doing it yourself—your conscience tells you that you are doing wrong. It makes you feel very unhappy. But if you do not listen to your conscience and lie about what you have done, your conscience becomes a little dull. The next time you do wrong, you cannot hear your conscience as clearly. You do not feel as unhappy. The more often you do not listen to your conscience, the duller it becomes. And after a while, it is of no use to you at all.

How can you keep your conscience sharp? Ask God to "direct your steps." That means, ask God to help you want to do right. Ask Him to help you keep from giving in to wrong thoughts, wrong words, and wrong acts. Then your conscience will stay as sharp as the sharpest knife. It will really give you a prick and make you feel bad every time you are tempted to do wrong.

11   "O TASTE AND SEE
THAT THE LORD IS GOOD"

How sweet are your words to my taste, sweeter than honey to my mouth.
—Psalm 119:103

When David, the sweet singer of Israel, sang about tasting the Lord's goodness, he was not thinking, first of all, about the food that goes into our mouths. He was thinking about God's Word. Listening to God's Word gave David as much pleasure as the eating of good food.

But we can also use David's words and mean the tasting of food. How will you act as you come to the breakfast table this morning? Will you pull up your nose at the food that will be waiting for you there? Are you a finicky eater? Do you make it difficult for your mother by always complaining about the food she gets ready for you each day?

There are very few foods that you cannot learn to like by trying a little every time they are served. It is all in the way you feel about it.

Trying new foods can be an exciting adventure. If you are taught as a child to eat whatever is served, even though it isn't your favorite food, you will save yourself a lot of trouble when you are older.

Eating is one of the greatest pleasures God has given us. Whenever we want to celebrate a happy event, like a birthday, we serve the most delicious food we know how to prepare.

Do you feel like praising God for His goodness when you sit down at your well-filled table? Step out into this new day with a thank-you on your lips and a song in your heart for God's wonderful gift of good food!

12   GOING NOWHERE

For everyone who calls on the name of the Lord will be saved. —Romans 10:13

Once there were two men who were going to travel to another city. They were going by train. But they didn't wait for the conductor to tell them where to go, or when to get on the train. They thought they could take care of themselves. They saw several cars of the train waiting on the tracks. So they went into one, found a comfortable seat, and were soon busy talking.

After a while a porter looked in and said, "You had better move into the car ahead."

But the men answered, "Why, what's wrong with this car?"

"Nothing at all," grinned the porter, "only it isn't hooked onto anything that will take you anywhere!"

Many people are like those two men. They think they will get to heaven without any help from anyone else. It takes power to move a train along the tracks. All the cars must be hooked onto a strong engine if they want to get anywhere. People need power and strength, too, to get them on their way through this life to heaven.

You know who that power is. It is Jesus. Jesus said, "I am the door. By Me, if any man enter in, he shall be saved" (John 10:9). You must know Jesus. You must know who He is and what He has done for you. You must believe that He died for you on the cross. You must let Jesus live in you.

> Into my heart, into my heart,
> Come into my heart, Lord Jesus.
> Come in today, come in to stay,
> Come into my heart, Lord Jesus.

13 "I AM SO GLAD
FOR THE COLOR OF THINGS!"

*Though your sins be as scarlet, they shall
be as white as snow; though they be red
like crimson, they shall be as wool.*
—Isaiah 1:18

What if everything in your home were a dull
gray? What if your living room had dull gray
walls and furniture, gray drapes, and gray carpet-
ing? How would it make you feel? Not very
cheerful, would it?

But remember, our God is a God of beauty.
When He planned this great world, He included
color. He gave us a whole rainbow of brilliant
colors!

Colors play a big part in your day. Soft
greens make you feel cool and restful. Bright
new spring-greens make you feel alive and full of
pep. They make you think of the coming alive
again of all God's creation. Yellow spreads cheer
and lightheartedness.

God must have loved blue—He gave us so
much of it! All the lakes and rivers and oceans
look blue. And what about the endless blue sky?
Blue is a beautiful color. Think of a baby's blue
eyes.

And what about brown—so rich, so soft, and

sometimes so good to eat! Who doesn't like a bowl of rich, chocolate pudding! And then there is black—it is soft, and rich, and beautiful, too. And it sets off the other colors so well. Think of a diamond pin on a black velvet dress.

And purple—that's a royal color! It makes you think of church and the sun shining through the purple of Jesus' robe in a stained-glass window. I like orange, too. It is so bright and cheerful, and it helps make food look interesting and good to eat. And then there is red—the most brilliant color of all. It makes you think of life itself, for our blood is red. And God says that our sins are red—deep red which we cannot clean away. But Jesus' red blood will take it all away, and make our hearts as pure as white snow!

14 THE ARTIST WHO FORGOT FOUR COLORS

Little children, you are of God—you belong to Him. —I John 4:4

Once there was an artist who was asked to paint a stained-glass window for a new church. The church was called "The Church of the Christ-Child"; so the people wanted a picture with children in it. First the artist painted the picture on a large white canvas. He made a lovely picture of Jesus with many children crowding around Him. The children looked so happy that it made the artist happy to look at them. He could hardly wait for the church committee to come the next morning to give their approval before he painted it on the glass.

But after he was in bed that night, he heard someone in his studio. He ran to look. There was a Stranger holding his color palette. The Stranger was painting on his picture! "Stop, stop!" the artist cried. "You are spoiling my picture!"

The Stranger turned to him and calmly said, "I am just making it right. Why did you use only one of your five colors for the faces of your children?"

The artist stammered. "I—I—just never thought about it."

The Stranger smiled, "Well, I have simply made some of the faces yellow, some brown, some black, and some red; for these little ones have come from many lands in answer to My call."

"Your call?" asked the artist. "What call was that, Sir?"

"Suffer the little children to come unto Me, and forbid them not, for of such is the kingdom of heaven," He said. Suddenly the Stranger was gone, and the artist awoke to find himself still in his bed. He rushed to his studio and worked on his picture. Now the children came from every land: some were Chinese, some African, some Indian. It was lovelier than anything he had ever made. And the committee was very pleased with it. One lady said, "Why, it's God's family at home with Him, isn't it?"

Are you a part of God's big family? Do you feel at home with your many brothers and sisters?

15 "GIVE, OH, GIVE AWAY!"

God loves a cheerful giver. —II Corinthians 9:7

> Give, said the little stream,
> Give, oh, give; give, oh, give;
> Give, said the little stream,
> As it hurried down the hill.
> I'm small, I know, but wherever I go—
> The trees grow greener still.
> Singing, singing all the day,
> Give, oh, give away.

Have you ever sung this song in Sunday school? It tells us something very important about God's world. Not only do the things in nature give beauty to man, there is also a giving and a sharing in nature itself. The streams give water where it is needed, the trees keep the soil from washing away with the rains. The sun gives warmth to everything that grows, and the birds eat the bad insects. We could go on and on.

We could not live for a day if nature did not share with us. Neither could we live without God's direct gifts that do not come to us through nature. Our very life is a gift of God. God gives us our growth, our health, our minds. Everything we have comes from God.

Then how is it that, though we are given so much, we do not like to give? Why is it so hard to say Thank-You? Why is it so difficult to share and give away? Every year our country sets aside a special day for Thanksgiving. God's people meet in His house to bring their thanks to Him. And they bring their gifts to Him—gifts to be shared with those in need. But why wait until Thanksgiving Day? Let us make every day a Thank-You Day. Ask yourself each night before you go to sleep, "What did I give away today?" Perhaps it will be a happy smile and a kind word to some unhappy person. Perhaps it will be a helping hand to someone in need. What are you going to give today?

16 TALKING TO A FRIEND

Evening and morning, and at noon, I will pray and cry aloud, and He will hear my voice. —Psalm 55:17

Do you know how to pray? Where did you learn? Is it easy to pray? No, praying is not easy. Praying is not something sinful man likes to do. When a person prays, he is really saying that he is nothing and that God is everything. People do not like to feel that they are worth nothing. They want to feel big and important. That is why there are so many people who do not want to be a Christian. They do not want to have anything to do with God.

But if you love Jesus and belong to Him, then praying is the most important thing you do each day. Prayer is first of all praising God for His greatness. You worship Him, you honor Him, you remember how very great He is and how very small you are. Prayer is also saying Thank-You. You thank God for taking such good care of you. You try to remember all the things He has done for you each day. And prayer is asking. You ask God to take care of all your needs, your troubles, your worries. And finally, prayer is intercession. That big word means praying for someone else. You bring all the needs and troubles of your friends and loved ones to God, knowing that He will take care of them, too.

How do you learn to pray? You learn by doing. The more you pray, the easier it will become, and the better your prayers will be.

Prayer is really like visiting with someone you love. The more you love Jesus, the happier you are to be able to pray to Him.

17 GOD'S WAY

For My thoughts are not your thoughts, neither are My ways your ways, says the Lord. For as the heavens are higher than the earth, so are My ways higher than your ways, and My thoughts than your thoughts. —Isaiah 55:8, 9

Good morning! "If it is a good morning, which I doubt." Those are the words of gloomy old Eeyore, Winnie-the-Pooh's donkey friend. I hope they aren't your words as you face this new day. Every morning should be a *good* morning. It is a new beginning. It is just as if we are given a fresh, clean piece of paper to work on each day. We do not have to use the messy one we spoiled yesterday. We may begin again. And with the help of our Great Teacher, Jesus, let's try to make this day like a good paper—one which will please everyone: our Teacher—Jesus, our friends, and ourselves.

It isn't easy to make every day a good day, is it? It all sounds very simple. You know Jesus is your Savior. You pray to Him. You ask Him to help you have a good day. You really want to be happy, to do what others want you to do, and to make others happy too. But sometimes things don't work out the way you planned. Now you are disappointed and unhappy. You don't feel like obeying your parents. You are cross with them, and they become angry with you. Soon the nice clean day you started out with this morning is all messed up. Why?

Remember God's words to us in our verse for today. God has promised to care for us, to give us everything we need, to help us become good Christians. But He didn't promise to do it our way. He has a wonderful plan for each one of our lives. If we are to become the great Christians He wants us to be, He is going to have to send us disappointments and troubles and sorrows. It is only when we learn how to act when things don't make us happy, that we can grow to be more like Jesus. God's plan for our lives is much better than our own. When we take what He sends in a good spirit, we will soon learn that His way brings us far greater happiness than our own way would have. It is much more fun to do what we're supposed to do than to disobey. Try it and see how happy it will make you feel.

18   GOD MADE ME SPECIAL

So God created man in His own image, in the image of God created He him. He created them male and female. And God blessed them. —Genesis 1:27, 28

Did God make people in the same way a factory makes cars? When the Ford Company makes a new model Ford, it makes hundreds, perhaps thousands at a time. Each one comes off the line exactly like the one before it. Each one has the same number of parts, the same kind of motor, the same finish.

No, God does not create anything on an assembly line. Did you know that there are no two leaves alike on any tree? There are no two blades of grass exactly alike.

No two people are alike either. You may have some things about you that are like your father, or your mother, or your brother, or sister. But you will not be exactly alike. Not even twins are alike in everything. It is wonderful that we are different. When God made you, He made you special. He knew exactly how He wanted you to be. He had that all thought out even before you were born. He had a good reason for making you as He did.

No two people are alike and no two people learn alike. But each one will get there in his own time. And God has given everyone something that he or she can do better than anyone else. Perhaps you are always ready to help when asked. Perhaps you have a friendly laugh that makes everyone feel good. Perhaps you are a good friend who knows how to share and be kind. Remember, God made you as He did because He wanted you that way! Aren't you glad you are you?

19 "SWEET LITTLE JESUS-BOY"

You shall call His name Jesus, for He shall save His people from their sins.
—Matthew 1:21

> Sweet little Jesus-Boy,
> They laid You in a manger. . . .

What do you think of when you hear the word *Christmas?* The very word makes you feel happy and excited, doesn't it? For most children, Christmas is the very best day in the whole year. The next-best day is your own birthday. Right? Birthdays are wonderful days. Everyone is so glad you were born and have now lived another whole year, that they feel like celebrating. We are happy for our life and for another year of blessings.

Christmas is a birthday celebration, too, you know. Christmas celebrates the greatest, the most important, birthday there ever was. Christ is the special name for Jesus. It means that He is a King. Many of our Christmas songs tell about the birthday of our King. The word *Christmas* means a celebration for Christ.

Many people do not even know that Jesus was born as a little baby in Bethlehem. They may sing about the Baby born in a manger, but they don't know who He is! They don't know why He was born. Will you help tell the Good News to those who don't know?

20 LITTLE THINGS

I am aware of all your good deeds—your kindness to the poor, your gifts and service to them; also I know your love and faith and patience. . . . —Revelation 2:18, 19, *The Living Bible*

> Little drops of water,
> Little grains of sand,
> Make the mighty ocean,
> And the pleasant land.
>
> Little deeds of kindness,
> Little words of love,
> Help to make earth happy
> Like the heavens above.

Why is it that when we think about growing up, we always want to be some great person who has done something that everyone talks about? We like to picture ourselves getting honor from the whole world for something we have done which no one else has ever done. We think that the only great people are those who get their names in the paper or who are seen on television.

Do you know that for every one person who is honored for something great he has done, there are hundreds, perhaps thousands, who are rated great with Jesus? Jesus is much more interested in the little things we do each day than the one great thing He may allow us to do for Him some day. Jesus told His people again and again that if they were not willing to do the little things for Him, they would never be ready to do great things for Him.

Is Jesus pleased with the little things you do?

21 CHASING AWAY THE SHADOWS

Until the day break and the shadows flee away. —Song of Solomon 2:17

Were you afraid of shadows when you were small? Are you still afraid of dark shadows? I know a fun pretend-story about a little boy who was very afraid of the dark. His name was Tommy. One night, when Tommy's mother and father were next door for a little while, and he was asleep in his bed, the wind rattled the shutters outside his window and woke him up. He looked around at all the dark shadows in his room, and screamed with fright. Alexander, his cat, who could see in the dark, quickly came to his rescue.

"Whatever is the matter?" Alexander asked. "Wild animals!" cried Tommy. "My room is full of them! I see a tiger, and a rhinoceros, and a gorilla, and a huge snake all curled up!" Alexander soon chased away his fears. Together they shone a flashlight on all the wild animals. To Tommy's great surprise, the tiger was his striped bedroom chair, the huge rhino was his bookcase, the gorilla was the light fixture hanging from the ceiling, and the snake all curled up beside his bed was his own clothing lying on the floor where he had left it. Tommy laughed with Alexander, and promised never to be afraid in the dark again.

Grown-ups think shadows are very beautiful. They add much to the beauty of God's great world. But there are some shadows that frighten even grown-ups. David talked about being afraid of the shadow of death. Sometimes when you look at something, you see its shadow before you see the thing itself. People say they are afraid of the shadow of death, because the shadow means that death itself is not far behind. But Christians have good news for frightened people. Christians do not have to be afraid to die. For them dying means going home to live with Jesus. It is the greatest thing that can happen to anyone. It is like saying good night here to all our loved ones, and then waking up in heaven to say good morning to Jesus up there!

22 "I WISH YOU GOOD LUCK"

And we know that all that happens to us is working for our good if we love God and are fitting into His plans. —Romans 8:28, *The Living Bible*

Have you ever heard anyone wish you luck as you were ready to do something? Sometimes we have to do something and we're not at all certain we know how; or we have to go somewhere and we don't know exactly what is going to happen. Then our friends say, "I wish you luck." You know what they mean. They are telling us they hope we will succeed in what we have to do. They are hoping everything will turn out all right.

The truth is, there is no such thing as luck. Things do not happen by chance. A Christian does not believe in luck. He knows that everything happens according to God's plan. God already has a plan for your life—from the day you were born to the day you go to live with Him in heaven. And God has told you in His Word that nothing will happen to you without His will. And He has also promised that He will make everything that happens turn out for your good. He will even use the bad things to make you a better Christian and to keep you closer to Him. He has not promised this to those who do not love Him; but if you love Jesus and believe that He is your Savior, you need never be afraid of "bad luck." You may trust in Jesus to help you do your very best, and then you will succeed.

23   WHAT'S IN A NAME?

And I will give him a white stone, and in the stone a new name written, which no man knows except he who receives it.
—Revelation 2:17

Do you like your name? Are you happy to raise your hand when your name is called? Does it make you feel good to hear your name spoken by others? Or do you hate your name? Are you ashamed and embarrassed to answer to your name in public?

In early days names were chosen because they had a meaning. The Bible name John meant "God is gracious." The name Theodore (or Ted) meant "Gift of God." When Jacob's wife, Rachel, was dying, she named her newborn son Benoni, which meant "Son of sorrow." But Jacob changed his name to Benjamin, which meant "Son of my right hand."

If we stop to think of why we like certain names and do not like other names, we will discover it is usually because we knew a person who was called by that name. If we liked the person, we like the name. The name makes us think of the person. If we want to be proud of our name, if we want people to like our name, we must be the kind of person people like to remember.

When your name is spoken, do people picture in their mind a kind, loving, and happy child? If you want to make a good name for yourself, let Jesus help you do it. Jesus has promised that if we win the fight against Satan, He will give us a beautiful jewel with a new name written on it; and it will be a surprise to everyone. Don't you wonder what your new name will be? I do.

24 CORONATION DAY!

So then the Lord Jesus, after He had spoken to them, was taken up into heaven, and sat down at the right hand of God. —Mark 16:19

If you were to turn on your TV some morning and hear someone say, "Today is Ascension

Day," would you know what they were talking about? I don't think you would, and neither would the grown-ups of the world who are not Christians. They would not know that Ascension Day must follow Easter as the third great "special day" of the church, or the first two special days, Christmas and Easter, would mean nothing. If Jesus had not gone back to heaven after He rose from the dead, His work would not have been finished. His Spirit would never have come to live in our hearts.

When we think of Ascension Day, we remember the disciples' last hours with Jesus. We "see" Jesus saying good-bye to His friends on the top of a mountain. We "see" Him putting His hands out over them to bless them, and then we "see" Him suddenly disappearing into the clouds. And we remember the angels' words: "This Jesus, who was taken up from you into heaven, will come again in the same way as you saw Him go into heaven."

But what do you suppose happened on the other side of those clouds? What took place as Jesus returned to His throne in heaven with the great news of His all-out victory over His fierce enemy, Satan? We were not invited to be there at that great celebration, but we can imagine a little of it. We have seen kings being crowned on TV. We call that a coronation. What a beautiful sight that is—with everyone dressed in sparkling jewels and lovely robes. And we see them put a golden crown on the king's head, and place a golden rod in his hand. But nothing could be as wonderful as when the angels led Christ to His own throne at the right hand of His heavenly Father. What a celebration that must have been, with hundreds of angels singing His praises, and the great King of heaven placing the crown of victory on His head! Can't you hear Jesus saying, "Now, Father, it is My wish that all My children who believe in Me may some day have heaven as their home and may share in My glory"? Aren't you glad there is an Ascension Day? Aren't you glad Jesus is your King?

25   IMITATE WHOM?

Christ also suffered for us, leaving us an example that we should follow in His steps. —I Peter 2:21

Even though you may not want to be like other people, you will have a hard time carrying out your wish. For children are born imitators. Many of the things you learned when you were small, you learned by imitating those around you. Imitating is one of God's gifts to you to make learning easy. It is much easier to learn how to make something by watching someone else make it than by reading the directions. You learned to walk and talk by imitating someone in your family.

Imitating is fun, especially when we are playing games. But did you know that sometimes you imitate others even though you did not plan to do it? Because there is sin in the world, it is much easier to imitate the wrong in other people than the good. God knows this, and that is why His Bible is filled with the stories of the good and the bad His people have done. He knows that we will imitate others. He tells us many times to imitate Christ, who is our very best example. But it is not easy to imitate Christ because He was perfect. He had no sin. So Paul tells us to imitate him because he had succeeded pretty well in imitating Christ. Jesus tells us to be like the prophets who were willing to suffer for God's sake. And Hebrews 11 gives us a long list of heroes who became great because of their faith. If you want to become a great hero of faith some day, listen to the stories of these great men in the Bible and try to be like them.

26 WRONG FRIENDS

Blessed is the man who does not walk in the counsel of the ungodly. —Psalm 1:1

Do you know what the psalmist meant when he wrote the words of our verse for today? He is telling us that it is not a very good idea to pal around with a boy or girl who does not believe in the Bible and who does not want to do the things the Bible teaches. Your un-Christian friend may have wrong ideas and may get you to do wrong things with him.

I once read a story about a boy named Bobby. His mother was a Christian and she had taught him that good boys obeyed their parents and were kind to others. One day Bobby found a new friend. His name was Gordon. Gordon was not a very good boy. When he called on the phone to ask Bobby to come to his house to play, mother was not very eager to say yes. "He does many things I do not want you ever to do," she said, "and I am afraid that if you play with him too often, you will soon be doing them, too."

"Oh, mother," Bobby said, "Gordon is a nice boy, and he's my friend. We won't do anything wrong." So mother gave her permission.

Gordon was a bad boy. He soon coaxed

Bobby to help him catch his neighbor's cat. His plan was to drown the cat and then lay him on the lady's porch. They couldn't catch the cat, but they did trample the neighbor's flowers. And when Gordon saw his plan wasn't going to work, he became so angry that he picked up a stone and broke her window.

Bobby was not very happy about going home that afternoon. He knew his mother had been right, and he was very sorry for what he had done. After his spanking, he asked his mother to forgive him; and he asked God to forgive him, too.

Be happy if your parents are careful about the friends you choose.

27   GRANDMA SMITH GOES HOME

And we are not afraid, but are quite content to die, for then we will be at home with the Lord. —II Corinthians 5:8, *The Living Bible*

Susie and her little sister, Joni, were all excited as they got off the school bus that warm spring afternoon. Grandma Smith was coming to their house and she was going to stay for a long time.

Grandma was old. She was so little and her face was full of wrinkles, but when she smiled her eyes lit up like twinkling stars. And her voice! Grandma had such a rich, clear voice. She told such wonderful stories about when mother was a little girl.

One afternoon the girls rushed in from school, calling, "Where's grandma? She promised to tell us the rest of last night's story." Mother sat down in grandma's chair and drew her little girls on her lap. "Grandma went home," she said softly. "Oh, I thought she was going to stay all summer," Joni said. Mother went on, "The angels came while she was napping and took her to her heavenly home. Now she and grandpa are together again, and they are very happy in their new home with Jesus."

Susie and Joni looked so surprised and disappointed that mother added, "Grandma told me this morning she couldn't wait for Jesus to call her home." "Did you see the angels?" Susie asked. "Was it hard to carry grandma all the way to heaven?" Mother smiled. "Grandma's body is still on her bed. She doesn't need it anymore. The angels took her spirit. We will bury her body. But when Jesus comes again, He will give her a new body which will never look old or get tired."

Then mother took the girls in to see grandma's tired old body which she had left behind. Susie looked for a long time. Then she said, "I am sad and I am glad at the same time. But I am mostly glad that grandma isn't tired anymore and is so happy with Jesus."

28 THE VINE AND THE BRANCHES

I am the Vine, you are the branches. He who abides in Me and I in him, he it is that bears much fruit, for apart from Me you can do nothing. —John 15:5

Jesus uses many ideas and word pictures to explain to His children the important truth that a Christian is one who lives in Jesus and has Jesus living in him. How is that possible? We do not know how it is possible, but we have Jesus' word for it that it is true.

One of the word pictures Jesus uses to make this clear to us is the picture of the vine and its branches. Do you know what a vine is? It is a plant that grows fruit, but it is not a tree. A vine's branches cannot grow out into the air by themselves. They cannot hold themselves up. They twine around a stick or a string, or they grow up the side of a wall, or they creep along the ground. Pickles and squash and melons grow on vines along the ground. Grapes grow on a fencelike frame which the farmer builds for the vine.

If you were to cut off a branch from the grapevine and plant it separately, it would not grow. It would die at once. The branch gets its life from the vine. It must remain a part of that vine if it wants to live and grow grapes.

We are just like that branch. Jesus calls Himself the Vine, and He says we are the branches. If we want to be alive Christians who bear fruit (do good things) for Jesus, we must let Jesus live in our hearts so that His life can flow through us and make our actions good fruit which He can use. Let's try to be good branches for His Vine.

29 BREAD

Jesus said to them, "I am the Bread of Life. He who comes to Me shall not hunger." —John 6:35

Another word picture Jesus uses to teach us what it means to be a Christian, is *bread.* Jesus used bread one day—five little loaves of it—to feed thousands of people. He worked a miracle on that bread so that it was enough for all those people.

Not long after Jesus had fed those five thousand men and their families, a big crowd gathered to listen to Him again. He said to them, "Did you come back to Me because you ate your fill of the bread I gave you? Don't waste your time on food which doesn't last. Ask for the Bread which lasts forever. The Son of God will give you this food."

Then the people asked Jesus, "What must we do to be a Christian?"

Jesus answered, "You must believe on Him whom God has sent."

Then they said, "What sign will you give us, what work will you do so we may believe? Moses gave our fathers manna, which was bread from heaven. That was the food they ate in the wilderness."

"Moses didn't give your fathers that manna," Jesus said. "It was God who gave the bread from heaven. And now He is doing it again. I am the Bread of Life. He who comes to Me will never be hungry!"

What did Jesus mean when He called Himself Bread? Bread is perhaps the most important food we have to eat. When we take it into our mouths and swallow it, it changes into different chemicals which our body needs; and soon it becomes a part of our bodies. It makes us grow and become strong.

When we take Jesus into our life, He becomes a part of us, too. He feeds our souls. He keeps us alive and strong and well. He is the only food our souls need to live forever.

Jesus wanted to be certain that His people never forgot this important lesson. On the night before He died, He took a piece of bread and broke it, and gave a piece to each of His friends. "Eat it," He said, "and remember and believe that My body was broken for you." God's people are still doing that in their churches. They call it "The Lord's Supper." When you are old enough, you may eat that bread, too, to show that you remember Jesus' death.

30   WHAT WILL YOU HARVEST?

Don't be misled [fooled] : remember that you can't ignore God and get away with it: a man will always reap just the kind of crop he sows. —Galatians 6:7, *The Living Bible*

If you lived on a farm, you would know that there are two seasons—spring and fall—which are very important and exciting. In the winter the farmer almost forgets that he is a farmer. His land looks hard and dead. Sometimes it is covered with snow. And the fruit trees stand bare in the orchard. In the summer the farmer can also take it a little easy. His hard work is over for a while. He can relax and enjoy the hot days and warm nights. He can sit back and watch God put the finishing touches on his hard work.

But in the spring and in the fall the farmer is a busy man! In the spring he plows his fields and makes the dry earth soft and pliable again. He makes up his mind what kind of food he wants to grow on his farm; then he goes out to buy the best seed he can find. And next he plants his seed. He is very careful to plant the seeds just right—not too deep nor too close to the surface; not too close together nor too far apart. All summer long he watches his seeds grow. Soon his fields look good with waving grain and ripening corn.

And then comes fall and the harvest. What an excitement as all the food is cut down and gathered in! Some is stored in barns for the animals, some is canned and frozen for the family, and some is brought to the market to be sold. The harvest time is a time of great joy.

Our life is something like a farmer and his

farm. We sow and harvest too. When we are children and young people we are constantly sowing. Our thoughts and our words and our actions are the seeds we sow. The harvest time will come when we are older and at the end of the world. And what will we harvest? Exactly what we sowed! A farmer never expects peas from corn seeds, or potatoes from cabbage seeds. He will not look for wheat if he sowed weeds. We will not be able to stand before God with our arms full of good fruit if we didn't sow any. Your actions now are very important. Let's be careful of our seed, shall we? Let's be sure it is good!

31 SUPERSTITIONS

And the Lord said, "Fear not, for I am with you and will bless you." —Genesis 26:24

Do you know what superstitions are? Perhaps you have never heard the word, but I think you know what it means. A person who is superstitious is always afraid bad things are going to happen to him because he has done certain things. He is like the little boy in the *Winnie-the-Pooh* stories, Christopher Robin. He was afraid that bears would come out to get him if he stepped on the cracks in the sidewalk. So he always stepped over the cracks.

Missionaries who go to bring the story of Jesus to the jungle tribes in Africa can tell you many stories about superstitious fears. I know a kind missionary grandmother who adopted 160 African babies in the years she lived there because their fathers were superstitious. When an African mother died, no one dared to touch the newborn baby. They believed that an evil spirit had killed the mother and was now in the baby. They were afraid the evil spirit would hurt them if they touched the baby. Before the kind missionary grandmother came to them, the babies were just left to die. But she taught them that Jesus loves their babies and wants them to live.

Aren't you glad we don't have to believe in superstitions? We know that nothing happens by chance. We know God has planned every detail of our lives. He knows what is going to happen to us long before it ever happens. And He has promised that we need never be afraid if we trust Him.

32 "BEHOLD, I STAND AT THE DOOR AND KNOCK!"

Behold, I stand at the door and knock; if anyone hears My voice and opens the door, I will come in to him and eat with him, and he with Me. —Revelation 3:20

When Jesus was here on earth, He was always explaining to people that He could not be their Savior unless they would let His Spirit come into their hearts. After Jesus had gone to heaven, He told His friend John to write a letter for Him to all His churches. Our Bible verse for today is a part of that letter. Jesus is still waiting to come into our hearts.

I still remember a song my sister sang when I was little. It was about the Holy Spirit wanting to come into a person's heart. He first went to a little child and pleaded to be let in. But the child said, "Oh, no, childhood is only for fun and play. Please go away. Some other day I'll ask you to stay." The Spirit came back when the child was grown. But he was still not ready. "Please go away," he said. "Life is too full of interesting things right now. Some other day." The Spirit came again and again, but each time the man sent Him away. He wanted to be a Christian, but it was never quite the right time. The Spirit came once more when the man was

57

growing old. "You are getting older," He said. "The years are now slipping by fast. You had better hurry while God's grace still lasts." "Oh, Spirit," he cried, "please go away. I am too busy and tired today. When I have time I'll bid you stay."

This is the way the song ended: "The old man now leans on his trembling staff, with a quivering, bitter sigh, 'I've wasted a lifetime in sin,' he cried, 'and now I am going to die. The Spirit, long slighted, has flown away, no hope, no God, I cannot pray; no other day, no other day, the Holy Spirit has gone to stay!' "

Jesus stands at the door of your heart today. Let Him in! Now is the best time of your life!

33   BUILDING ON A ROCK

What then of the man who hears these words of Mine and acts upon them? He is like the man who had the sense to build his house on rock. The rain came down, the floods rose, the wind blew and beat upon that house; but it did not fall because its foundations were on rock. —Matthew 7:24, 25, *The New English Bible*

58

And that Rock was Christ. —I Corinthians 10:4

Have you ever watched a carpenter build a house? Where does he begin? He must first find a strong, solid place on which to build. Then he digs a big hole for the basement. He makes wooden forms for the walls of the basement and pours cement into the forms. When the cement is dry, he takes away the wooden forms, and the cement walls are like solid rock. And on this strong foundation he builds his house.

Jesus knew about the need for solid foundations, too. He talked about the wise man who built his house on rock. The rain and the wind and the storm could not break down that house. But there was a foolish man, too. He built his house on the sand. It was a beautiful house. It looked lovely; it had everything a man could want. It looked just as strong as the wise man's house. But oh, oh, when the storm came! The wind and the water washed away the sand beneath the house, and it toppled and fell. The man's work and money were wasted; there was nothing left!

Jesus says that all people are like either the wise man or the foolish man. If we live our life without Christ, if we do as we please and do not listen to the words of Jesus, we are like the foolish man. We will lose our life forever, as the man lost his house. But if we listen to the words of Jesus and do what He says, we will be like the wise man. No matter what bad things may happen to us, our life will last for all eternity.

Christ is our Rock! Not only is He the strong foundation on which we build our life, He is also our hiding place. Others may fall against that Rock and get hurt, but we may hide in its shadow!

34 YES AND NO

Say just a simple "Yes, I will," or "No, I won't." —Matthew 5:37, *The Living Bible*

Yes and *no* are two of the smallest words in the English language. But they are, perhaps, the most important words in any language. When you were very small, these two words were among the first ones you learned to say. Little children go through a stage when they say no to everything: "No, I don't want my milk," "No, I don't like potatoes," "No, I don't want to go to bed," "No, I won't stop banging my little hammer on the table leg." A baby's *no* must be gradually changed to *yes* if he is to be a happy member of his family. He has to learn when to say no and when to say yes.

It isn't just the baby who has to learn this important lesson. All children and grown-ups have to learn it, too. *No* is such a little word—it is easy to spell, it is easy to write, and it is easy to understand. But why is it so difficult to use? As you meet with your friends today, in the classroom or on the playground, will you be able to use this little word when you should? If someone suggests that you play a mean trick on a pal, will you be able to say "No, I will not do such a thing"? If you are tempted to cheat in your work today, will you be able to say no to that temptation?

Sometimes *yes* is almost as hard to say as *no*. If you are being questioned about something wrong you have done, are you brave enough to step right up and say, "Yes, I did it"? Dare you stand up in a crowd and say, "Yes, I am a Christian," or "Yes, I love the Lord Jesus"? Think about these words today, and use them correctly.

> "N-O" is just a little word,
> And so is "Y-E-S."
> But, oh, the difference they do make,
> No one could ever guess.
> Say "N-O, N-O" to everything that's wrong,
> And "Y-E-S" to the Savior Jesus
> All day long.

35   SUNDAY

This is the day that the Lord has made;
we will rejoice and be glad in it. —Psalm
118:24

Do you think it was Sunday when the psalmist sang Psalm 118? When the psalms were written, the special day which was set aside for worship was Saturday. In Bible times the people worshiped on Saturday because God chose that day for them. God took six days to create the world and everything in it. Then He rested on the seventh day and made that the day of rest.

But when Jesus rose from the dead, He rose on Sunday. And when He sent His Holy Spirit to live in the hearts of His followers, He sent Him on Sunday. So the new church—Jesus' church—chose Sunday as their day of rest and worship.

We could sing the psalmist's song every morning, because every day is a day that the Lord has made; and we should be happy as we begin each one. But we should be specially happy on Sunday. If we were to remember every Sunday morning that on another Sunday morning, long ago, there was an empty tomb and Jesus rose from the dead so He could be our Savior, we would want to set this day aside as a special day. We would want to spend time in worship and praise to that wonderful Savior!

Oh, I know, church services are long and it isn't easy to sit still without talking for such a long time. But did you know that Jesus wants you in His Father's House, and is happy to meet with you there? He helps children sit still and get something out of the services. It gives you a good feeling to worship God with your family and friends. It helps you feel that you are a part of Jesus' church too. Even though you can't understand everything that is said, you will come away with a blessing. Jesus has promised it.

36   PUTTING THE BLAME
ON SOMEONE ELSE

Don't accuse anyone of what you know he didn't do. —Luke 3:14

Putting the blame on someone else for something you have done is as old as sin itself. Adam and Eve, the first people God created, had always been perfect. They had never done anything wrong. They never said anything wrong; they never even thought anything wrong. But when Satan came into the Garden of Eden and tempted Eve to disobey God's important rule, and Eve listened to Satan and ate from the forbidden tree, sin came into the world. From that day on, it has always been much easier to sin than to do right.

And when God came into the garden that day and accused Adam and Eve of disobeying Him, they didn't want to take the blame. Adam tried to blame Eve and God. He said, "The woman *You* gave me made me do it." And Eve blamed the snake.

It is still the same today. It is much easier to try to get out of admitting the wrong we did by blaming someone else, than to say, "Yes, I did it. It was all my fault." We know we will be punished for what we have done; so we quickly try to shift the blame. But deep in our heart we know where the blame lies, don't we?

Another wrong which we so easily fall into is to blame someone else when we don't even know what happened. When you can't find your rubbers as you are dressing to go home from school, or when your box of crayons is lost, what do you say? Isn't it usually, "Someone took my rubbers!" or "Someone stole my box of crayons"?

Try hard today not to blame anyone for your own faults or carelessness.

37 NO, NEVER ALONE

"I will never leave you, nor forsake you." —Hebrews 13:5

> No, never alone,
> No, never alone;
> He promised never to leave me,
> Never to leave me alone.

Have you ever sung this chorus? Does it mean anything to you? Ever since man left the beautiful Garden of Eden, where he was perfectly at home with God and could walk and talk with Him as a friend in the garden, people have always had times when they were lonely and afraid.

It begins already when we are babies. Babies cry when they are left alone. Little children are afraid to go to bed alone. They want mother to leave a light on so they will not feel alone. Even though boys and girls, like you, are too old to be afraid in the dark, they still have a fear of being alone. How often don't you feel slighted by your friends. Perhaps they have planned to do something and have not invited you. Perhaps you were not chosen to be a part of a ball game. You felt lonely and unwanted.

But you don't have to be lonely. Remember the Friend who stands at your heart's door and knocks! Jesus has promised He will *never* leave you alone! No matter where you go, no matter what you have to do, Jesus is always with you. No matter what your friends may do to you, no matter what may happen to you in life, you always have Jesus. And Jesus will turn your loneliest moments into times of greatest joy. If Jesus is your Friend, you need never fear loneliness again!

38   YOU DO NOT HAVE TO SEE GOD TO KNOW HE IS THERE

The ends of all the earth shall see the salvation of our God. —Isaiah 52:10

Is it hard for you to believe something you have never seen? It is true, most people want to see for themselves before they will believe what they are told. Jesus' friend, Thomas, was that way. He was so sad on that first Easter morning that he wouldn't even meet with the rest of his friends for prayer and worship. And so he missed seeing the risen Lord! Several days later, he was still walking around with a long face, when he met the disciples. They were filled with joy. "We have seen the Lord!" they shouted. But Thomas said, "Unless I can put my fingers in the nail-holes in Jesus' hands, and put my hand in His wounded side, I will not believe!" Jesus was kind enough to show His hands and side to doubting Thomas so he could believe. But Jesus said, "You believe because you could see; blessed are those who believe without seeing!"

We do not have to see God to know He is there. Have you ever seen the wind? No, you haven't; but you have no doubt at all that it is there when it carries your kite high into the air. Can you see the electricity as it comes through the wires and brings heat and light into your home? Why do you believe in electricity? Because you see what it does.

No, we cannot see God. He is a Spirit. He has no body. But we know He's there, all right. All we have to do is look at what He has made and what He does. Who but God could make this wonderful world of ours! Who but God could give life to plants and animals and you! Who but God can take such perfect care of everything He has made!

39 RUNNING TO WIN

*I have fought the good fight; I have
finished the race; I have kept the faith.*
—II Timothy 4:7

Have you ever run in a race? It's fun at a
picnic to take part in the games, isn't it? But
does everyone get a prize? No, only the one who
runs the fastest gets the prize. Then why try, if
you aren't at all certain you will win? But that
isn't the way champions talk, is it? They do not
know if they will win the prize, but they want
that prize, and they are going to try their very
best to make sure they get it.

In the days when Jesus lived, people ran
races with lightning-fast horses and chariots.
Those who took part in this race would stand in
their two-wheeled wagons and guide their horses
around the track. Sometimes these men wanted
to win so badly, they wouldn't play fair. They
would put sharp spears on the wheels of their
chariot, and then they would run too close to
the other chariot so they could break its wheel.
The charioteer would be thrown from his chariot and would often lose his life when that
happened.

The apostle Paul knew about those races. He
knew about the races where a man ran on a race
track to win a prize, too. Perhaps he sat in the

great stadiums of that day and watched the races, as we do today. Paul thought of his own life as a race. He worked as hard as he could. He did the very best he knew how to do. And he kept his eye on the goal, which was heaven. When his life was almost over, he said, "I have fought the good fight; I have finished the race; I have kept the faith." No laziness for Paul, no unfair fighting, no cheating. He had done his best, and he was satisfied.

Are you a good runner?

40 BEGINNINGS

Thy mercies are new every morning.
—Lamentations 3:23

What do you think of when you hear the word *beginning?* This word brings to mind many things, doesn't it? Perhaps you go way back to the very first verse of the Bible, where we read, "In the beginning God created the heavens and the earth." That was the beginning of everything. But the world is full of beginnings—the beginning of you, for instance, on the day you were born. And on every birthday you begin a new year of your life. Then there is the beginning of a new school year, when you start a new grade, or the beginning of vacation when you do not have to go to school.

Time is divided into beginnings and endings, too. Each day has its beginning and ending. So does each week and each month. Even the years are divided in the same way. Each year begins in January and ends in December.

When each new year begins, people like to make what they call New Year's resolutions. That means they promise themselves that they are going to stop doing certain things and begin to do other things in the new year. When the new year begins, what kind of promises could you make? What things are you going to try not to do? Do you tattle on your brothers or sisters or friends when they are doing something you think is wrong? Do you play too rough and hurt other children? And how about some things you can try to do, such as being more kind and obedient and loving? Remember that Jesus is there at the beginning of every new time with His help; so you will be able to keep your promises!

41   FLAG WAVING

Give honor and respect to all those to whom it is due. —Romans 13:7

I think it is a wonderful sight to look up toward a beautiful, deep blue sky and see my country's flag waving in the breeze! It makes me feel good to see my country's flag flying free in front of my house.

What do you think of when you see your country's flag flying above you? Why is it that when a man carries the flag in a parade, everyone honors it? Why do people raise their right hand in salute to the flag? Is it such an important piece of cloth?

The cloth in a flag is no different than the cloth in a girl's dress or a boy's shirt. The United States flag is made up of strips of red and white cloth sewed together with a square of blue cloth on which white stars are placed. A flag is important because it stands for something. When you look at a flag, you think of the country that owns it. When you honor the flag, you are honoring the country to which it belongs. When you mistreat the flag—when you tear it, or burn it, or drag it through the mud—you are showing hatred for your country.

We know that America is not perfect. We know that our leaders do not always do their best. We know that some people in our country are not treated as kindly as they should be. We are sorry when this happens, and we pray that God will help our leaders to be fair and kind to everyone.

But God has been very good to us. We live in perhaps the greatest country in the whole world. Our country is rich. We have more than we need of everything. And we do share what we have with other countries. We send food and medicine where they are needed. We send men and women to other countries to show people how to be good farmers. We send nurses and doctors to teach people how to take care of their sick. And we send missionaries all over the world to bring the story of Jesus to all men.

So let us be proud of our country. Let us do our share to make it a better country. The next time you see your country's flag, honor it, and say a prayer for your country. Ask God to make it the best country in the world for Him!

42   HAPPINESS AND JOY

Whoever trusts in the Lord, happy is he.
—Proverbs 16:20
In thy presence is fullness of joy. —Psalm 16:11

Do you know what happiness is? Do you know what joy is? Charlie Brown's little friend, Linus, thinks happiness is having a soft blanket to hold. Many little children are like Linus. Why do you suppose a blanket gives happiness to a small child? Perhaps it reminds them of how safe they feel when their mother snuggles them into their cribs at night, tucking the blanket right up under their chin.

The word *happiness* really comes from the word *hap,* which means "chance" or "luck." But today it has come to mean "feeling good, being cheerful, feeling glad." When you are glad, you are excited. You want to clap your hands, you want to skip and shout.

Joy, however, is a feeling that goes deeper than happiness and gladness. Joy can fill your heart to overflowing. When you have joy, you are perfectly satisfied.

When something bad happens to you—perhaps you are sick and have pain, or you fell and hurt yourself—you do not feel happy at all. But you can still have joy in your heart even when you are unhappy. "How is that possible?" you ask. True joy is something Jesus gives. When you have His joy in your heart, it is there to stay.

Happiness and joy are two great gifts of God. The Bible tells us that if we trust in God we will be happy. It also tells us that true joy comes when we are in the presence of the Lord. That means that if Jesus lives in our hearts, He will fill us with His joy.

43   MY MOTHER!

Honor your father and your mother, that your days may be long in the land which the Lord, your God, gives you.
—Exodus 20:12

When you were a baby, one of the first words you learned to say was *mother,* or *mama. Mamma* is the easiest word for a baby to say, and it's the word he wants to say most often. No one is as close to you as your mother. Before you were born you were a part of your mother. No wonder a baby wants to be close to his mother! He feels best when she has her arms around him, hugging him tight.

And when you began to grow up and were no longer a baby, who took your hand and helped you to walk? Who fed you your food until you learned how to feed yourself? Who took care of you every day? Your mother! Why do you suppose mothers are willing to spend so much time with their children? Why are mothers so concerned about what happens to their children? Why? Because that's what it means to be a mother! That's what a mother is. That's what a mother does.

Most children, especially if they are Christian children, never forget their mothers, even when they are grown up and have become mothers and fathers themselves. They come back home again and again to visit their mothers. They show her how thankful they are for all she has done for them. To them every day is Mother's Day, because they honor their mother every day. When the five girls in the contest for Miss Universe this year were asked, "If you could be someone else, whom would you choose to be?" one of them said, "My mother! She is the most wonderful woman in the world." I hope you feel that way about your mother!

44   NIGHT

In the night His song shall be with me.
—Psalm 42:8

Are you glad that God made the night? Are you glad that every day is divided into daytime and nighttime? Sometimes, when we're having a lot of fun, we wish night would never come, don't we? But if we had to stay up all day and all night without resting, we would soon know how wise God was in giving us the night.

In its own way, the night is as beautiful as the day. On a clear night, the sky is one of God's great wonders in His creation. The millions of stars look like tiny diamonds sparkling on a black velvet robe. The Milky Way looks like a long, long road you could ride straight to the throne of God. And when the moon shines, the whole dark world seems to glow and sparkle. Have you ever walked in your own backyard when it was turned into a fairyland, by a full moon shining on new-fallen snow? The night is truly beautiful.

But most of the time we don't see what is going on in the night, do we? We are fast asleep in bed. Going to bed should be the happiest time of the day. It is the time when mother or daddy takes time out to be alone with you. They read to you or tell you stories. They pray with you. It is the time when God comes very close to His children. And when you are left alone, what do you think about? Try to remember all the good things that happened during the day. Try to plan something you could do tomorrow to make someone happy. Sing a song to show your love to Jesus before you fall asleep. Then it will truly be a *good night.*

76

45 "WHITER THAN SNOW"

But now your sins are washed away, and you are set apart for God. —I Corinthians 6:11

Do you like to play in the snow? I think it is one of the best "fun things" a child can do. Snow is so beautiful. It comes down so softly. It is fun to watch it glide gracefully through the sky. And it does such a good job of covering up a dirty world! Snow is just as beautiful at night as it is in the daytime. With the help of street lights, or the moon, the snow dresses the trees and shrubs in sparkling jewels. And the evergreen trees look lovely in their new furry coats.

When I see the new-fallen snow, I cannot help but think of God. Today man has succeeded in making artificial snow. But it costs many dollars and takes time to make enough snow to cover one ski hill. In one hour, God can cover a whole city!

Snow also makes me think of God's words to us. My little pupils in kindergarten love to sing:

I learned it in the Bible,
A tender little prayer,
And when snowflakes are falling
So beautiful and fair,
I say to my dear Savior

This little prayer I know—
"Wash me and I shall be whiter than snow."

Yes, the Bible tells us that our hearts are not clean. They are filled with sin. But Jesus can wash them and make them even whiter than the pure snow! And He washes them with His own red blood. When Jesus died on the cross, His blood took away our sins and made our hearts clean.

The next time you see the lovely snow come drifting down, won't you say this little prayer, too? And then thank Jesus for making your heart clean.

46   WHEN I GROW UP

Let us please God by serving Him with thankful hearts. —Hebrews 12:28

Some children know what they want to be when they grow up before they are even old enough to go to school. Perhaps a little boy has an uncle who is an airplane pilot, and being able to pilot a plane looks like fun to him. Perhaps a little girl has a friendly neighbor who is a nurse and who knows just what to do when someone gets sick. So being a nurse looks good to her. Some children are very good with pets. They love animals and seem to know just what to do when an animal needs help. They may grow up to be an animal doctor.

But most children haven't any idea what they want to be when they are grown. When boys see a policeman, they think that is what they want to be; or when they see a fireman, that looks good to them. And all little girls picture themselves being a mother with babies to take care of.

The world needs people who will be good leaders, who know how to run things. We need great doctors, great scientists, great teachers, great business men and women. But those who become great just to honor themselves will not do the world much good.

You will naturally choose something you are good at doing, something you know you will be able to do well. But if you are a Christian, you will try to find the work which will help you serve God. Then you will not only succeed in what you are doing, but you will be pleasing God at the same time. You do not have to worry about what you are going to do. God has a plan for your life. He knows how you will be able to serve Him best. Just ask Him to show you as you grow older what His plan is. He will do it.

47 "COUNT YOUR BLESSINGS"

And it is He [God] who will supply all your needs from His riches in glory, because of what Christ Jesus has done for us. —Philippians 4:19

Are you the kind of child who looks at his pal's belongings and says, "His is much better than mine"? Do you have to make certain that your piece of cake is just as big as your brother's or sister's? It is so easy to feel sorry for ourselves, isn't it? That is something every Christian has to fight every day of his life. Even fathers and mothers find it easy to feel sorry for themselves. But it isn't a good thing to do. In fact, it is sin; and it doesn't help anyone to be a better Christian.

In the first place, the things we tell ourselves when we feel that way are usually not true. We tend to exaggerate. Perhaps one girl has a better dress than you have and you wish you had that dress. Then you tell your mother, "Every girl in my room dresses better than I do!" Or perhaps your friend's dad took him to a ball game and you are jealous; so you tell your dad, "I'm the only boy in my room who can't go to ball games with his dad!"

In the second place, when we feel sorry for

ourselves, we make ourselves feel miserable, and we make everyone else feel miserable, too!

I know a song which is very good to sing when you start feeling sorry for yourself. It is called "Count Your Many Blessings." Have you ever tried doing just that? You don't think you have any blessings? Think again. Count on your fingers all the blessings you can think of. The more you think, the longer your list will grow. Soon you will have more blessings than fingers. When that old "feeling-sorry-for-yourself" ache starts to bother you again, get out your fingers and count. You will be surprised at what the Lord has done!

And what will your fingers of blessing include? Your father and your mother and a family who loves you. A good home with all the comforts of life. Two eyes to see. Two good legs to carry you where you want to go. But don't stop there. Keep on going. Your list will never end!

Since we respect our fathers here on earth, though they punish us, should we not all the more cheerfully submit to God's training so that we can begin to really live? —Hebrews 12:9, *The Living Bible*

When Johnny was asked what he wanted to be when he grew up, he immediately answered, "I want to be a father!" That's a good answer, isn't it? What better wish could anyone have than to be like his father!

A home that is complete must have a father, a mother, and some children. Some homes have no father—just a mother and some children. Some homes have no mother—just a father and the children. And sometimes there is only a husband and a wife, but no children. If you belong to a complete home, you should be very thankful.

Sometimes we think of a home as a complete circle, with every one holding hands. The mother's hands are soft and tender. They hold the circle together with much love and kindness. The father's hands are firm and strong. They protect the home and keep fear and want out.

Children do not see as much of their father as they do of their mother. It's the mother's job to take care of her children all day long. The father takes good care of his children, too, but in a different way. God planned it so. The father must go away from home each day so that he can work and earn money for his family. The father must see to it that his family has a house to live in, and food to eat, and clothes to wear. He must provide money for doctors and dentists. He must pay for his children's education. He must see to it that the city they live in is a good city. He must help make this world the best place it can be for children to grow up in.

So your father is a very busy man. But he has another job which is also very important. God gave him this job, too. He must train his children to love God and to do His will. He must teach his children how to love all men and how to show that love in kind deeds. And he must punish his children when they do wrong, so they will grow up to be good. The word *father* is such a wonderful word that God chose it to describe Himself. He is our Father. He can make us really live!

49 JESUS AND THE CHILDREN

But Jesus said, "Let the little children come to Me, and don't prevent them. For of such is the kingdom of heaven."
—Matthew 19:14, *The Living Bible*

Sometimes children feel sorry for themselves. They feel as if no one pays any attention to them. The world seems to be "For Grown-Ups Only." If the children who feel that way could take a look at the children who lived long years ago, they would change their minds. In the days when Jesus lived, parents loved their children; but they didn't think children were very important. Children were not allowed to talk when grown-ups were present. They sat perfectly quiet at the table and did not say a word. They were never asked what they wanted. They were told what to do and when to do it. Boys were more important than girls because boys would grow up to be men. Some fathers who were not Christians would not even let their wives keep the baby if it was a girl. Boys and girls were often sold as slaves and made to do hard work for long hours each day. And they were whipped and beaten very often.

But when Jesus came, all this changed. Jesus knew that His heavenly Father loved the children. They were His, too, because He had made them. As soon as Jesus began His work as a minister, He showed His love for the children. He always took time to touch the sick children and make them well. He walked many miles to go to the bedside of Jairus's daughter. She was dead, but Jesus made her live again.

One day when some men asked Jesus about the kingdom of heaven, Jesus called a little boy to come to Him. He put His arms around him and said to the men, "Unless you become trusting and loving like this little boy, you'll never even get into God's kingdom."

Another time, Jesus was sitting at a well, talking busily with some important men. Some mothers with their children joined the group. The children tried to push their way to Jesus, and the men tried to shoo them off. But Jesus stopped talking to the men. He said, "Make room for the children. Don't send them away. They belong to the kingdom of heaven, too." Then the children ran to Jesus. They climbed on His lap. Jesus put His hands on their heads and blessed them.

Jesus loves you, too. You are very important to Him. He died to save you!

50 THE LOST SHEEP

If a man has a hundred sheep, and one wanders away and is lost, what will he do? Won't he leave the ninety-nine others and go out into the hills to search for the lost one? And if he finds it, he will rejoice over it more than over the ninety-nine others safe at home. —Matthew 18:12, 13

Have you ever seen a shepherd taking care of his sheep? Many children living in America have never seen a shepherd. But in the land where Jesus lived, it was a very common sight. There were many, many shepherds in Jesus' day. And you will still find them there today. When I was in Galilee, I saw a shepherd leading his sheep up the mountainside in Nazareth.

When Jesus wanted the people to understand how very much He cared for His own people, He told them the story about the lost sheep. There was this shepherd who had a hundred sheep. And this shepherd knew every one of those sheep. He even gave them names. And when he called them by name, the sheep would come running.

All day long the shepherd would lead his sheep. He brought them to a good place to eat grass. He brought them to quiet streams of water so they could drink their fill. He led them up mountains to find more grass. He let them rest in a shady place. And when evening came, he would bring them back to the sheepfold. And each night he counted his sheep to make certain they were all there.

One night the count was short. There were only ninety-nine! One was gone. But why bother? He had ninety-nine. Wasn't that enough? But where was the one? Who wants to go out into the storm to find one lost sheep? The shepherd did, because he loved that sheep. So he braved the storm and went out to look. Up and down the hills he went, calling, calling. Finally, between loud thunder crashes, he heard a faint "Baa-Baa!" And in the flash of the lightning, he saw his sheep, caught in the bushes! How eagerly he went to get him! How carefully he carried him home! What happiness in the family circle that night when he told about the sheep that was lost! How the shepherd loved his sheep!

And what did Jesus say about all this? "Even so, the angels in heaven shout for joy when one of My little ones comes to Me!"

51 SPECTACLES

And Jesus said, "Go and tell John what
you see: the blind receive their sight."
—Matthew 11:5

When Jesus walked on this earth, He was the greatest doctor that ever lived. He spent much of His time healing the sick. And He did not have to work the way doctors do today. He did not have to study and experiment to try to find medicines and cures for sicknesses. He could make sickness go away with a touch or a look or a word.

Jesus still heals today. When we are sick, we pray to Him to make us better. And He does this by helping the doctor know what is wrong and what to use to cure it. Sometimes He works miracles today, too, and cures people without the help of a doctor.

Once there was a little boy in India whose name was Rama. His father was a goldsmith who made beautiful patterns on gold bracelets and necklaces. But Rama's father had a bad pain in his eyes and soon he could not see to do his work. So there was no money and no food. Rama's mother said, "But what can we do about it? It is the will of the idols!"

Rama decided to go once more to pray to

their idol. The only gift he could bring was a little water in his brass bowl. He brought it to the temple and sprinkled it over the idol. "Give back my father's eyes, O, Vishnu," he begged.

As he was lazily walking home, he heard some strange singing and saw a crowd of people listening to a man talking. This man was a missionary. Rama had never seen a white man before; so he pushed through the crowd and got up right close to him. He liked what the man was saying, but he had to laugh at the queer pieces of glass the man had fastened on his nose! He had never seen jewelry like that before. So he called out, "Sahib, why do you wear that glass on your nose?" The missionary said that his eyes once were very sore and he couldn't see clearly, but as soon as he looked through those pieces of glass, called spectacles, his eyes didn't hurt anymore and he could see perfectly. Rama quickly told the missionary about his father and begged him to come to his house.

Of course the missionary went with Rama. Soon the missionary made plans to take the whole family with him to his hospital. Rama's father was operated on, and later he was given glasses, or spectacles, too. Jesus had helped the missionary to give sight to the blind!

52 DON'T WAIT UNTIL
YOU ARE GROWNUP

Therefore, as the Holy Spirit says, "To-
day, if ye hear His voice, harden not
your hearts." —Hebrews 3:7

Today is the most important day in your whole life! It is the only day that is really yours. Yesterday is gone, and tomorrow—well—no one is certain about tomorrow. Tomorrow may never come. But we do have today. So it is very important to do our very best today.

Do you remember Rama, the little boy from India whose father needed spectacles? Today I want to tell you about his sister, Amanda. Amanda was left at school when their mother and father went back to their old village after the father's eyes were cured. Amanda wanted to learn how to read. She was a proud little girl. She wanted everyone in the village to praise her for being so bright and for being the only girl who could read. This wasn't a very good way to feel, and Amanda thought so herself before long.

You see, she began to watch the missionaries at the school, as well as some of the little girls who were now Christians. They were quite different from the girls she knew. They were kind to each other. They didn't mind eating less food so Amanda could stay at school. They never grabbed for things that didn't belong to them. And they never bragged.

"When I grow up, I'm going to be just like those Christian girls," Amanda told the missionary one day. "Don't wait until you are grown up," the missionary said. "The only time to begin is right now! So put your wish to work, dear." "I will," Amanda promised.

The very next day, another little girl came to school. She wanted to stay so badly, but there was no more room. The father begged, and the little girl cried, but still there was no more room.

Amanda went to the missionary and offered to give up her place to the new girl. "I was the last one you squeezed in," she said, "and I have already learned the alphabet." But the other girls cried, "No, no! Why should Amanda go? We will all squeeze a little more and eat a little less." And they did. And there was more love in everybody's heart because Amanda was so kind to the little girl who almost had to be turned away.

Be like Amanda. Don't wait until you are grownup to be kind. Be kind today.

53 "I WANT A PET!"

And David said to Saul, "Your servant kept his father's sheep, and there came a lion and a bear, and took a lamb out of the flock. And I went out after it, and struck it, and delivered the lamb out of its mouth." —I Samuel 17:34,35

Tommy was going to be six in a few days. Whenever anyone asked him what he wanted for his birthday, he would always say, "I want a pet." Tommy had had several small pets in the past. He loved animals and was always begging for one. He always promised to take good care of his new pet. But Tommy wasn't very good at keeping his promises. He would be very careful the first few days; then he would forget and his pet would die. He left his turtle in the hot sun for a whole day. The water dried up in the pan, and his turtle died. His gerbils were fun to have, too. His mother warned him to watch them closely if he wanted to keep them. But, once again, Tommy forgot. He left the door of the cage open one day and the gerbils ran away. He never found them again.

Tommy's last pet was a beautiful parakeet, and he loved him very much. It was fun to try to teach him how to talk. But Pretty Boy never learned a word because Tommy didn't have the patience to try over and over again. It was fun, too, to take him out of the cage and let him fly around the room. Then Tommy would hold out his finger and Pretty Boy would sit on it and let Tommy put him back in the cage. But one day Jeff came over to play. They took Pretty Boy out of the cage and began chasing him around the house. The game got more and more wild until the little bird was almost frantic. Mother scooped him up with her soapy hands and put him back in the cage. But the next morning Pretty Boy was lying dead in the bottom of the cage.

Now Tommy was going to be six, and he was begging again. The night before his birthday daddy was reading the story of young David, the shepherd lad, who took care of his father's sheep. When father read about the lion and the bear coming after the lamb, Tommy's eyes grew big with wonder as he pictured the brave David rescuing his lamb from those fierce animals. Tommy sighed, "I wish I was as good with animals as David was."

"Now that you are going to be six," father said, "perhaps you can learn to be." So Tommy got another pet. This time it was a puppy—the cutest little cocker spaniel you ever saw! And Tommy tried hard. He never again forgot to take good care of his pet!

54 TIME

My times are in Your hand. —Psalm 31:15

Isn't time wonderful? It is one of the best gifts God gave us. We would not know how to live without time. We would not know when to get up, or when to go to school, or when to eat if there were no time. The farmer wouldn't know when it was spring and time to plant, or when it was fall and time to harvest. We would not be able to make any plans. How could we plan meetings, or picnics, or camping trips if we didn't know about time?

When God made the sun and the moon, He made time, too. He planned for days and nights, for winter and summer, for worktime and playtime. Once time seemed to stop for a whole year. In the days of Noah, when people were very wicked, God sent a big flood to cover the whole earth. The only people who did not drown were Noah and his family. They were safe in the big boat God helped Noah build. It was called an ark. After the rain stopped, the ark just floated around on the water for almost a year. There was no spring, or summer, or fall, or winter. There was just one boat with eight people in it, plus many animals and birds, on an earth that had turned into one huge ocean of water.

But when the water had dried up, and Noah and his family could live on the dry land again, God gave them a promise. He said, "As long as the earth remains, seed-time and harvest, cold and heat, summer and winter, and day and night shall not cease."

God has shown us how to break up time into smaller parts, too. The days are divided into hours and minutes and seconds. Seconds are very short. Just one count and a second is gone. Minutes aren't much longer. Count to sixty slowly, and a minute has gone by. There are sixty counts, or seconds, in a minute; and there are sixty minutes in an hour. Hours make up days and nights. And so time goes on.

We will have time as long as this world lasts. But one day Jesus will come on the clouds of heaven. And that will be the end of time. Then we will live with Jesus in His heavenly home, and we will have no need for time. We will live there forever.